Ladybird Readers

Amazing Predators

Inspired by BBC Earth TV series and
developed with input from BBC Earth
natural history specialists

 To download full story audio in both British and American accents, and to complete
the listening activities at the back of the book, visit **www.ladybirdeducation.co.uk**

Contents

Picture words

cheetah

polar bear

leopard

frigate bird

Parson's chameleon

dorado fish

praying mantis

blue whale

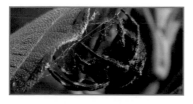

Darwin's bark spider

Chapter One
Predators and Prey

All animals need to eat to live. Some animals eat other animals, so they must find and catch their food before they can eat it. They are **predators***, and the animals they eat are their **prey**.

cheetah

gazelle

This cheetah is a predator. The gazelle is its prey.

*Definitions of words in **bold** can be found in the glossary on pages 63–64

Ladybird Readers

Amazing Predators

Series Editor: Sorrel Pitts
Written by Cheryl Palin

LADYBIRD BOOKS

UK | USA | Canada | Ireland | Australia
India | New Zealand | South Africa

Ladybird Books is part of the Penguin Random House group of companies
whose addresses can be found at global.penguinrandomhouse.com.
www.penguin.co.uk   www.puffin.co.uk   www.ladybird.co.uk

Penguin
Random House
UK

First published 2018
001

Printed in China

A CIP catalogue record for this book is available from the British Library

ISBN: 978-0-241-33618-2

All correspondence to:
Ladybird Books
Penguin Random House Children's
80 Strand, London WC2R 0RL

MIX
Paper from
responsible sources
FSC® C018179

Many different kinds of animals are
predators or prey. They can be big or small.

Spiders, like this
little Darwin's bark
spider, are predators
that **hunt** insects.

Some birds, like this
frigate bird, are predators
that hunt fish.

Predators and their prey live in very different **habitats** all over the world.

Some habitats, like jungles and rainforests, are very warm. The Parson's chameleon hunts large insects in the forest.

Other habitats, like the **Arctic**, are very cold. Here, polar bears hunt seals on the sea ice.

Not all predators hunt on land. The world's biggest predator is the blue whale, and it hunts its favorite prey, krill, in the sea.

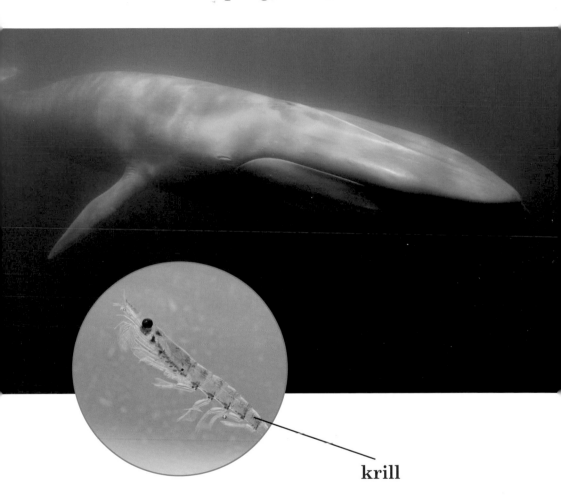

krill

Life is not easy for predators. Their habitats give them different challenges, so they all have different ways to hunt.

Chapter Two
Cheetahs

Cheetahs live on the **grasslands** of Africa. They hunt and eat large animals, like gazelles and young wildebeest.

Cheetahs don't only hunt food for themselves. This mother has four hungry young cheetahs that need a big meal every day.

It is not easy for cheetahs to hunt on the open grasslands. There are not many trees or plants, so there is nowhere for cheetahs to hide from their prey.

Wildebeest are also difficult to hunt, because they are so heavy and strong.

Cheetahs have a special **skill** which helps them to hunt. They are the fastest predators on land. They can run at 93 kilometers per hour, but they can only run this fast for ten seconds, so they must **stalk** their prey until they get very near. Then, they can run!

This cheetah can only hunt a young wildebeest. The cheetah is not very heavy, so it cannot jump on the wildebeest to catch it. It must try to make the wildebeest fall down on the ground.

This time, the young wildebeest has escaped.

Cheetahs are excellent at hunting, but they don't always catch their prey.

CHAPTER THREE
Leopards

Not all big cats hunt in the same way.
Leopards cannot run as fast as cheetahs,
so they need to catch their prey differently.

The colour and pattern of their fur gives them **amazing camouflage**, which helps them to hide.

Leopards also have a special skill—they can move very slowly and quietly to hunt their favorite prey, impala. The leopard must get very near to this impala before it is seen.

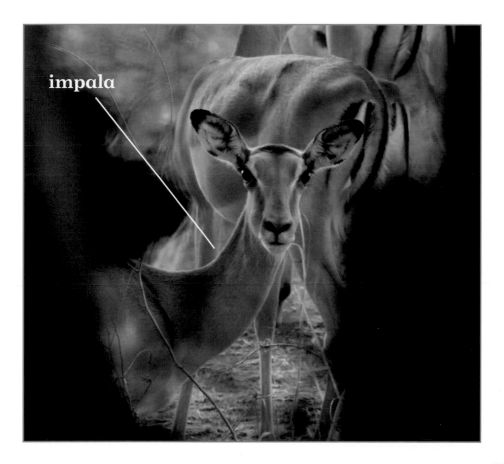

impala

Sometimes, leopards must hunt impala out in the open, so they must be very clever to find a place to hide and stalk their prey.

These impala haven't seen the leopard, because it's hiding in the lower ground. Can you see it?

When the leopard is close enough, it runs and catches an impala. Then, it pulls its prey down to the ground.

FACT

Leopards only catch their prey once out of every seven times they hunt!

The leopard has had to be very patient, but now it can eat.

CHAPTER FOUR

Parson's Chameleons

Not all predators are big animals like cheetahs and leopards.

This predator is a Parson's chameleon, and it's about the size of a house cat. The Parson's chameleon lives in the forests of Madagascar, and its prey is insects.

Insects are not easy to catch, so the chameleon must not move quickly because the insects will run or fly away. To help it find and hunt its prey, the chameleon has special eyes. It can move each eye in all directions, so it doesn't need to move the other parts of its body.

Some insects have special skills, too. Stick insects use camouflage, so it's difficult for predators to know what is a stick, and what is a stick insect.

Chameleons can only see their prey when it moves, so until the insect moves, the chameleon cannot see it.

Luckily, chameleons have another unusual body part to help them.

A chameleon's **tongue** is longer than its body, and it can move very fast to catch an insect.

When the tongue catches the insect, it cannot get away.

CHAPTER FIVE
Praying Mantises

Some insects are predators, too.
This praying mantis lives in the jungle.
It's an insect, but it also eats insects.

FACT

Praying mantises sometimes
eat other praying mantises!

A praying
mantis has five
eyes—two large
eyes, and three small
eyes between them.

It also has amazing front legs. The legs move
very quickly to catch prey, and they also
have **sharp** parts, so the prey cannot escape.

Like the Parson's chameleon, the praying mantis can only see its prey when it moves.

It can see very small movements, so when this insect moves, the praying mantis immediately catches it with its sharp front legs.

Some kinds of mantises look like flowers, and they use their amazing camouflage to hunt their prey. They climb a plant until they reach the flower, and then they wait. As soon as an insect lands on the flower, they catch it!

CHAPTER SIX

Darwin's Bark Spiders

Spiders also catch prey. The Darwin's bark spider is a very small predator, which lives along the rivers of the rainforest in Madagascar.

FACT

The body of a female Darwin's bark spider is 18—22 millimeters long, but a male's body is only 6 millimeters long!

This female spider eats the insects that fly down the river. It is difficult to catch this prey, but the spider has an amazing skill. She can produce very long lines of **silk**.

The wind carries the lines of silk across the wide river to make an enormous, 25-meter bridge! It is hard to believe that such a small spider can make so much silk!

The silk is very unusual, too. It is much **tougher** than the silk of any other spider.

The Darwin's bark spider then makes a web on the bridge. Its web is called an orb web.

The Darwin's bark spider makes the biggest orb webs in the world.

An orb web made by a Darwin's bark spider can be two meters wide.

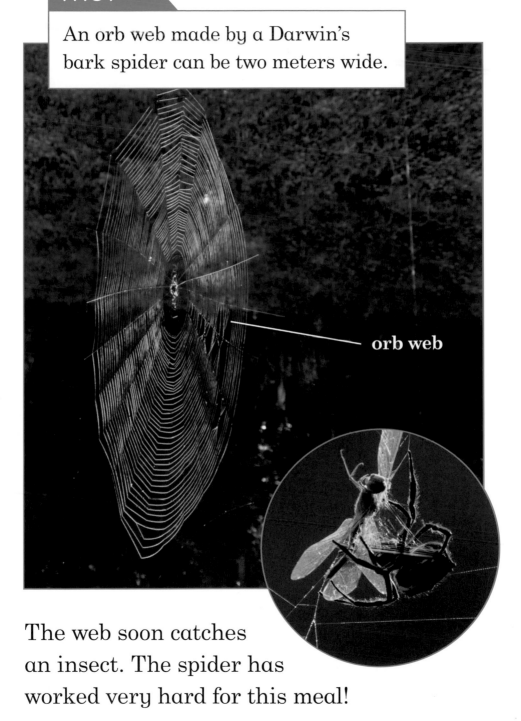

orb web

The web soon catches an insect. The spider has worked very hard for this meal!

Chapter Seven
Plant Predators

Insects are not always the prey of other animals. Some unusual plants are predators, too.

This plant, which grows in wet habitats, is called a sundew. The **soil** is not very good here, so the plants also need to catch insects for food.

The plants have leaves with tentacles, and each tentacle has **liquid** on the end. This liquid smells sweet to some insects.

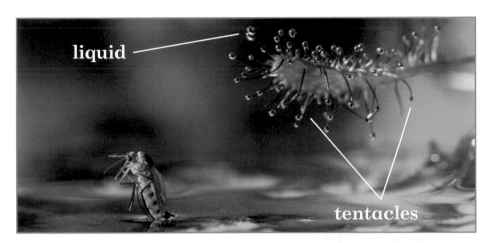

liquid

tentacles

The liquid is very sticky. When a mosquito touches the liquid, it cannot escape.

When it tries to move, it touches more liquid, which makes it harder to get away. Soon, it becomes the plant's food!

The Sundew is not the only plant predator.

This plant is a Venus flytrap. The inside of the flytrap is pink, and it has a sweet liquid around it. Flies see the colourful plant, and want to drink the sweet liquid.

flytrap

The flytrap also has lots of small hairs inside it. If a fly touches two of these hairs in twenty seconds, the flytrap closes, and the fly cannot escape.

The plant eats the insect, and then it opens again to catch more prey.

CHAPTER EIGHT
Polar Bears

The cold Arctic is home to polar bears, and it is a very challenging habitat. The ice is always changing, and this makes finding food difficult for these big predators.

Polar bears hunt seals, but during some months it is very difficult to find any seals. A polar bear must get very near to a seal before the seal sees it. To do this, the polar bear swims between holes in the ice.

Often the seal escapes.

At the end of spring,
it is warmer, and there
is not as much ice.
The polar bear must
find a new way to hunt.

It swims in the sea until
it notices a seal.
It does not swim too
near, because the seal
might smell it. Then,
the polar bear suddenly
surprises its prey!

Seals can swim very well, so polar bears cannot usually catch them underwater, but this polar bear is lucky. It has caught the seal in the water! It's only a small seal, but it's enough food for the polar bear for one week.

CHAPTER NINE

Frigate Birds and Dorado Fish

Some animals must travel a long way to feed. Frigate birds often fly more than 100 kilometers before they find food. They eat fish, but they must not go too close to the 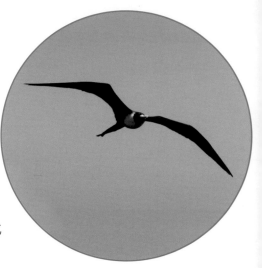 water. Their **feathers** are not like other seabirds' feathers—they must not get wet.

Frigate birds need help to hunt their prey.

These dorado fish are one of the fastest **ocean** predators. They look for food near the top of the water and, like frigate birds, they eat smaller fish.

Under the water, the little fish try to hide from the dorado fish, but it isn't easy. The little fish have an unusual way to escape . . .

. . . they **glide**! If the wind is behind them, these fish can move for hundreds of meters through the air.

This is what the frigate birds were waiting for! When the fish glide too high, the birds fly down to catch them, and when the fish jump back into the sea, the dorado fish eat them.

This is how frigate birds and dorado fish help each other to catch their prey.

CHAPTER TEN

Blue Whales

The ocean is also home to the largest predator in the world. The blue whale is thirty meters long. It's the biggest animal that has ever lived—bigger than the biggest dinosaur!

FACT

A blue whale's tongue **weighs** the same amount as an elephant!

Blue whales are excellent swimmers.
They need to be good at swimming, because
they often have to travel a long way under
the water to find enough food.

The ocean's biggest animal eats one of the
ocean's smallest animals—krill.

krill

FACT

Krill are smaller than
your little finger.

The blue whale opens its large mouth, and fills it with krill and **seawater**. The whale takes in so much seawater that it weighs twice as much as normal, and it has to take a break from swimming!

This part of the whale is full of water!

Then, the whale uses its tongue to move the water out of its mouth.

The strong hairs inside the whale's mouth stop the krill from escaping. This means the blue whale can eat a lot of krill at the same time.

CHAPTER ELEVEN

Amazing Predators

The Earth's predators have to work very hard to eat and to live in their challenging habitats.

Often, large areas of the sea offer no food for blue whales and frigate birds, so they must travel a long way to hunt.

The changing ice in the Arctic creates problems for polar bears.

In the open grasslands, it is difficult for a stalking leopard to hide.

Prey also have some surprising ways to escape from their predators.

Stick insects use camouflage to hide from the animals that hunt them, like chameleons.

Flying fish jump out of the water and glide on the air to get away from hunting dorado fish.

Although hunting is difficult, predators have amazing body parts that they use to catch food. For example, when an insect is caught by a praying mantis' sharp front legs, or the long, sticky tongue of a Parson's chameleon, there is no escape!

Predators also have many wonderful skills to help them catch their prey.

The Darwin's bark spider can create the world's biggest orb webs.

The cheetah is the world's fastest animal on land.

Our planet's predators really are amazing!

Activities

The activities at the back of this book help you to practice the following skills:

✏️ Spelling and writing

📖 Reading

💬 Speaking

🎧 Listening

❓ Critical thinking

✴️ Preparation for the Cambridge Young Learners exams

1 **Read the sentences. If a sentence is not correct, write the correct sentence in your notebook.** 📖 ✏️

1 Predators are animals that don't eat other animals.

2 The animals that predators eat are called prey.

3 Frigate birds are predators that hunt insects.

4 Predators live in warm and cold habitats.

5 The world's biggest predator is the blue whale.

6 Predators all hunt in the same way.

2 **Read the definitions. What is the correct word for each one? Write the words in your notebook.** 📖 ✏️ ❓

1 a place where an animal or plant is usually found   **h** . . .

2 to follow and catch animals for food   **h** . . .

3 an animal that hunts other animals   **p** . . .

4 an animal that gets hunted by other animals   **p** . . .

5 the part of the world which is furthest north, where it is very cold   **A** . . .

3 **Match the two parts of the sentences.**
Write the full sentences in your notebook.

1 Cheetahs hunt and eat large animals,

2 On the grasslands, it is difficult for

3 Cheetahs stalk their prey, and then

4 Cheetahs are excellent are hunting, but

a they run very fast to catch it.

b like gazelles and wildebeest.

c they don't always catch their prey.

d cheetahs to hide from their prey.

4 **Read Chapter Two. Then, read the**
answers below, and write the questions
in your notebook.

1 They live on the
grasslands of Africa.

2 Because they are so
heavy and strong.

3 At 93 kilometers
per hour.

4 For only ten seconds.

5 Read Chapter Three. Are sentences 1—5 *True* or *False*? If there is not enough information write *Doesn't say*. Write the answers in your notebook.

1 Leopards can run at 93 kilometers per hour.

2 A leopard's fur helps it to hide.

3 Leopards like to hide behind big trees.

4 Leopards catch their prey every time they hunt.

5 Leopards can run faster than cheetahs.

6 Leopards must move very slowly and quietly when they hunt their prey.

6 Talk to a friend about the animals below. How are they the same? How are they different?

Cheetahs live in the grasslands of Africa. Leopards . . .

7 **Choose the correct answers, and write the full sentences in your notebook.**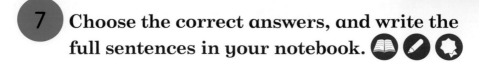

1 The Parson's chameleon is the same size as . . .
a a leopard. **b** a cheetah.
c a big cat. **d** a house cat.

2 What does the Parson's chameleon eat?
a insects **b** birds **c** fish **d** cats

3 What can a chameleon move in all directions?
a its head **b** its legs **c** its feet **d** its eyes

4 What does a stick insect use to hide from predators?
a noise **b** special eyes
c camouflage **d** its legs

8 **Choose the correct words, and write the full sentences in your notebook.**

1 **Not all / All** predators are big animals.

2 The Parson's chameleon lives in the **seas / forests** of Madagascar.

3 Insects are **easy / not easy** to catch for a chameleon.

4 Chameleons can only see insects when they **move. / jump.**

9 **Look at Chapter Five. Ask and answer the questions with a friend.** 💬

1

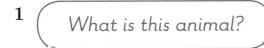

> *What is this animal?*
>
> *It's a praying mantis.*

2 Where does it live?

3 What does it eat?

4 What is special about praying mantises?

5 How do praying mantises hunt their prey?

10 **Complete the sentences using words from Chapter Five. Write the full sentences in your notebook.** 📖 ✏️ 🏵️

1 The praying mantis can only see its prey . . .

2 Some kinds of mantises look like . . .

3 They use their amazing camouflage to . . .

4 As soon as an insect lands on the flower, . . .

11 **Listen to Chapter Six. Answer the questions in your notebook.** 🎧*✏️

    1 Where does the Darwin's bark spider live?

    2 Which is bigger—the male spider or the female spider?

    3 What does the female spider make to catch its prey?

    4 What is special about the silk made by the Darwin's bark spider?

    5 What is the name of the Darwin's bark spider's web?

12 **Read the text. Find the mistakes, and write the correct sentences in your notebook. There are five mistakes.** 📖 ✏️

The Darwin's bark spider is very big. The female spider catches insects that swim down the river. She makes very short lines of silk. The wind carries the silk across the forest to make a bridge. The spider then makes a web on the bridge. The web catches birds for the spider to eat.

13 Choose the correct words, and write the full sentences in your notebook.

1	rocks	plants	trees
2	birds	chameleons	insects
3	plant	tentacle	leaf
4	sticky	sweet	hot
5	water	habitat	food

1 Some unusual . . . are predators, too.

2 The sundew catches . . . for food.

3 Each . . . has liquid on the end.

4 The liquid is . . . , so an insect can't escape.

5 Then, the insect becomes the plant's . . . .

14 Write a description of how the Venus flytrap catches its prey. Draw some pictures to help with your description. Write in your notebook.

The inside of the Venus flytrap is . . .

15 Look at the picture and read the questions. In your notebook, write the answers as complete sentences.

1 Where is this polar bear?

2 Is the habitat of polar bears warm or cold?

3 Why is the Arctic a challenging habitat?

4 Which animals do polar bears hunt?

16 Listen to Chapter Eight. In you own words, describe how polar bears hunt for food. Write in your notebook.

*To complete this activity, listen to track 9 of the audio download available at **www.ladybirdeducation.co.uk**

17 **Write the answers to the questions in your notebook.** 📖 ✏️ 💬

1 Which animals help the frigate birds to hunt their prey?

2 How far do frigate birds often fly to find food?

3 Why can't the frigate birds go too close to the sea?

4 Where do dorado fish look for their food?

5 How do the dorado's prey escape from them?

6 What do the frigate birds do when the little fish glide too high?

18 **Read the text, and write all the text with the correct verbs in your notebook.** 📖 ✏️

A dorado fish . . . (**look**) for food near the top of the water. A little fish tries to escape by . . . (**glide**). It can . . . (**jump**) out of the water and glide for hundreds of meters.

When the little fish glides too high, a frigate bird . . . (**fly**) down to catch it. If the little fish . . . (**jump**) back into the sea, a dorado fish . . . (**eat**) it.

19 **Answer the questions. Write full sentences in your notebook using the words in the box.**

> thirty meters   dinosaur   krill   mouth
> krill and seawater   tongue

1   How big is the blue whale?

2   What do blue whales eat?

3   Why does the blue whale get very heavy when it eats?

4   What does the whale use to move the water out of its mouth?

20 **Talk to a friend about blue whales. Ask and answer questions.**

> Where does the blue whale live?

> It lives in the ocean.

> What is special about the blue whale?

> Which animal weighs the same amount as a blue whale's tongue?

21 Read the information. Choose the correct words, and write them in your notebook. 📖 💭

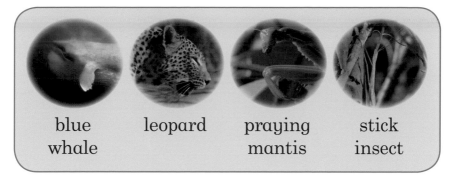

| blue whale | leopard | praying mantis | stick insect |

1 This animal catches prey in its sharp front legs.

2 This animal tries to hide from its prey.

3 This animal travels a long way to hunt.

4 This animal uses camouflage to hide from predators.

22 Write a short story or poem about one of the predators in this book. Write it in your notebook. ✏️ ❓

Project

23 Look online or in a library, and find out about another animal that is a predator.

Make a presentation about your predator. Work in a group. Include the information below:

- What is the animal called?

- Where does it live?

- How big is it?

- Which animals does it eat?

- How does it hunt?

Glossary

amazing *(adjective)*
Something that makes you feel surprised and happy is *amazing*.

Arctic *(noun)*
the part of the world furthest north, where it is very cold

camouflage *(noun)*
the way an animal's colour matches its habitat, which makes it difficult to see

feather *(noun)*
birds have many of these soft, light things on their bodies

glide *(verb)*
to move through the air, a bit like flying

grasslands *(noun)*
a large area of land with lots of wild grass

habitat *(noun)*
a place where an animal or plant is usually found

hunt *(verb)*
to follow and catch animals for food

liquid *(noun)*
something that isn't a hard object or a gas (e.g. water or oil)

ocean *(noun)*
the water that goes across most of the Earth

predator *(noun)*
an animal that hunts other animals

prey *(noun)*
an animal that gets hunted by other animals

seawater *(noun)*
water from the sea

sharp *(adjective)*
having a thin edge that
can cut or make a hole
in something

silk *(noun)*
a soft, light material

skill *(noun)*
to be able to do
something well

soil *(noun)*
the part of the Earth
in which plants and
trees grow

stalk *(verb)*
to follow slowly and
quietly

tongue *(noun)*
the soft part that moves
around inside the
mouth, which is used for
tasting and speaking

tough *(adjective)*
something that is not
easy to cut or break

weigh *(verb)*
to find out how heavy
someone or something is

Visit **www.ladybirdeducation.co.uk**
to choose your next book!